SO YOU THINK YOU KNOW?

ABERDEEN

Produced by The Francis Frith Collection
exclusively for

OTTAKAR'S

www.ottakars.co.uk

First published in the United Kingdom in 2005 by The Francis Frith Collection®

Hardback edition published in 2005 ISBN 1-84567-787-0

British Library Cataloguing in Publication Data

So You Think You Know? Aberdeen
Text adapted from original material supplied by Norman M Miller

The Francis Frith Collection
Frith's Barn, Teffont,
Salisbury, Wiltshire SP3 5QP
Tel: +44 (0) 1722 716 376
Email: info@francisfrith.co.uk
www.francisfrith.co.uk

Printed and bound in England

Front Cover: **ABERDEEN, UNION STREET c1900** A90309t

The colour-tinting is for illustrative purposes only, and is not intended to be historically accurate

CONTENTS

ABERDEEN, THE ALBERT MEMORIAL PRE 1873 SA000007

(Courtesy of University of St Andrews Library)

ABERDEEN MISCELLANY

The earliest royal charter was granted to Aberdeen in 1179.

The first Aberdonian whose name we know was Ricardus Cementarius. He was also the first known civic head (aldermanus).

Aberdeen paid a higher feu duty on its Freedom Lands than any other Scottish burgh, except one: Berwick-upon-Tweed.

Provost Sir Robert Davidson died while leading the men of Aberdeen in the battle of Harlaw in 1411.

Aberdeen's first university was founded in 1495.

By 1593, Aberdeen had two universities, the same number as England.

By 1528, Aberdeen had two bridges over rivers. At the time, this was almost as remarkable as having two universities.

In the Civil War, Aberdeen was always on the wrong side, being controlled by Royalists when the Covenanters were winning and by Covenanters when the Royalists were winning.

One of the worst atrocities of the Civil War was the massacre of civilians in Aberdeen in 1644, by Cromwell's New Model Army.

George Jamesone (1588-1644), Scotland's first great painter, was born in Aberdeen. He painted portraits of prominent local people, and also royalty.

ABERDEEN, THE FISHING FLEET 1895 SA000040 (Courtesy of University of St Andrews Library)

ABERDEEN, IN UNION TERRACE GARDENS c1900 A90311

Ptolemy, the 1st-century Egyptian cartographer, mentions a place which could be Aberdeen on his map of the world. He calls it 'Devana'.

The Artist George Jamesone's daughter, Mary Jamesone, embroidered five large tapestries, four of which survive in the Mither Kirk of Aberdeen (see page 4).

Between 1423 and 1635, eleven provosts of Aberdeen were called Menzies, most of whom served more than one term.

The Menzies (see above) were Roman Catholics, which would normally exclude them from public office. They kept quiet about it and so did everyone else.

ABERDEEN, THE HARBOUR c**1900** A90312

Aberdeen solicitors (uniquely) call themselves advocates.

James Gibbs, one of Britain's greatest architects, was born in Aberdeen in 1682. His best-known work is St Martin-in-the-Fields in central London.

Returning home in 1739, James Gibbs (see above) was made a freeman and gave his native city plans which were used for rebuilding the West Kirk.

During the '45 Jacobite rebellion, Aberdeen was occupied successively by both sides. The city's Hanoverian friends treated the citizens worse than their Jacobite enemies.

In 1767 Marischal Street was laid out on a viaduct along all its length. It was probably the first example of the urban flyover.

ABERDEEN, THE SWAN POND, DUTHIE PARK c**1900** A90315

ABERDEEN, MUNICIPAL BUILDINGS 1880 SA000004

(Courtesy of University of St Andrews Library)

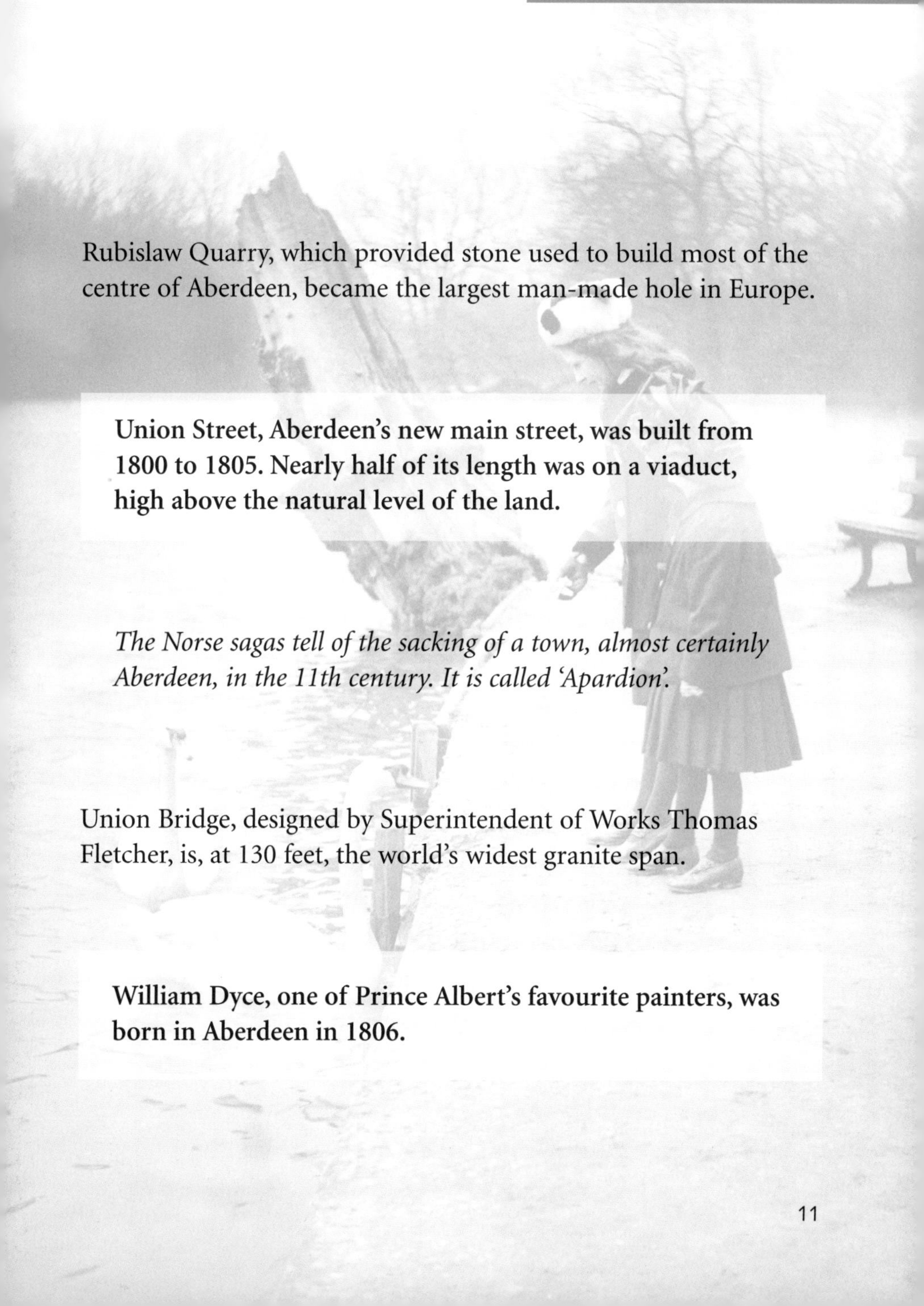

Rubislaw Quarry, which provided stone used to build most of the centre of Aberdeen, became the largest man-made hole in Europe.

Union Street, Aberdeen's new main street, was built from 1800 to 1805. Nearly half of its length was on a viaduct, high above the natural level of the land.

The Norse sagas tell of the sacking of a town, almost certainly Aberdeen, in the 11th century. It is called 'Apardion'.

Union Bridge, designed by Superintendent of Works Thomas Fletcher, is, at 130 feet, the world's widest granite span.

William Dyce, one of Prince Albert's favourite painters, was born in Aberdeen in 1806.

Aberdeen produced several noted artists in the 19th century, including William Dyce (see page 11), James Giles, John (Spanish) Philip and Sir George Reid. Aberdeen is the only local council in Scotland ever to have declared itself bankrupt. This occurred between 1821 and 1828.

The Aberdeen company Alexander Hall and Co built the first of the Scottish clippers, 'Scottish Maid', in 1839.

ABERDEEN, THE FISH MARKET c1900 A90316

ABERDEEN, MARISCHAL COLLEGE c1900 A90318

Alexander Hall and Co (see page 12) also built the first vessels in the Japanese navy.

'Thermopylae', the fastest of all clipper ships, was built by Walter Hood's yard in Torry in 1859.

The railway reached Aberdeen in 1850, providing a through route all the way to London.

ABERDEEN, THE ALBERT BASIN AND THE FISH WHARF 1902 SA000039
(Courtesy of University of St Andrews Library)

ABERDEEN, UNION STREET 1878 SA000005 (Courtesy of University of St Andrews Library)

A scheme to provide a secure supply of clean water to Aberdeen opened in 1866, starting at Invercannie, over 20 miles from the city. The waterworks and the reservoirs are still used.

Following the success of Union Street, several other viaduct streets were built, making Aberdeen one of the most heavily engineered of British cities.

The Great Charter was granted to Aberdeen by Robert the Bruce in 1319.

Trams first ran in Aberdeen in 1874. Two routes served the main shopping streets.

Trawl fishing came to Aberdeen in 1881, with the arrival of 'Toiler'.

Aberdeen's covered fish market was built in 1886 and was to become the largest in the world.

The first photograph of the moon was taken from Skene Terrace in Aberdeen.

The Aberdeen universities were united in 1860, but the burghs were only united in 1891.

The world's longest tunnel for mains electric cables is in Aberdeen.

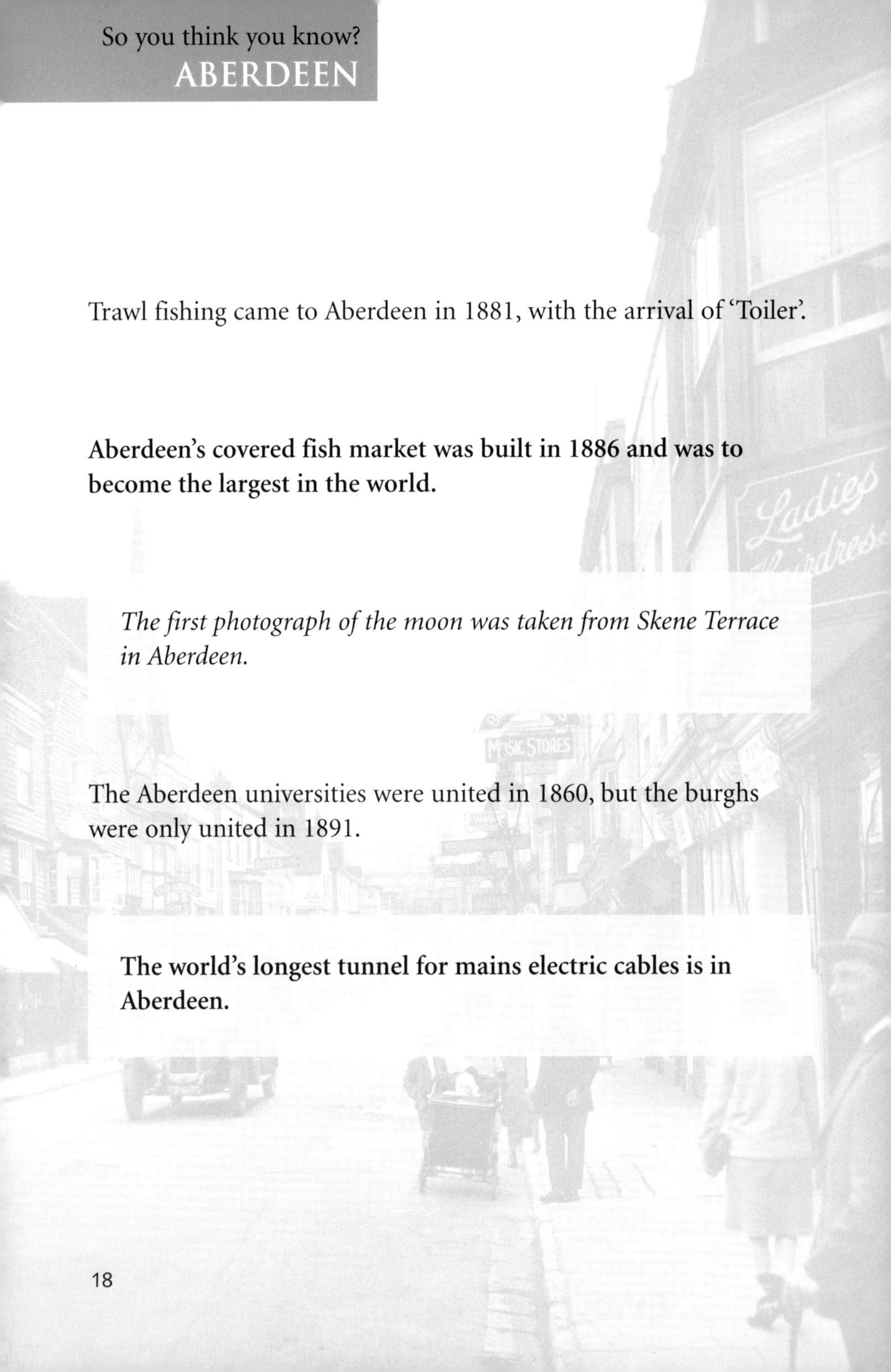

ABERDEEN, GORDON'S COLLEGE 1889 SA000031

(Courtesy of University of St Andrews Library)

ABERDEEN, UNION STREET LOOKING WEST 1938 SA000013
(Courtesy of University of St Andrews Library)

Aberdeen was the destination for the world's longest scheduled races between railway companies. The trains started in London.

Aberdeen Suburban Tramway Company was probably the smallest operator of street tramways in Britain.

During the First World War, three ships were built of concrete in Torry.

Britain's first iron lung was built in Aberdeen's City Hospital in 1933.

ABERDEEN, UNION STREET 1938 SA000014
(Courtesy of University of St Andrews Library)

Dr John Boyd Orr, who established his reputation at the Rowett Research Institute near Aberdeen, was appointed first head of the UN Food and Agriculture Organisation, and was awarded the Nobel Peace Prize.

Aberdeen was one of only a few places where the main roads into the town were picketed during the General Strike of 1926.

A Luftwaffe plane containing the secret 'Liechtenstein' equipment (the German equivalent of radar) landed at Dyce Airport in 1943, helping the RAF to win the war in the air. By studying this equipment the British were able to perfect their own radar system.

1945 saw the start of building of the council housing scheme at Kincorth, the last large-scale use of granite in the Granite City.

ABERDEEN, THE FREE SOUTH CHURCH AND PUBLIC LIBRARY 1892

SA000020 (Courtesy of University of St Andrews Library)

ABERDEEN, CASTLE STREET AND THE RAG FAIR c1900 SA000028

(Courtesy of University of St Andrews Library)

The magnetic resonance imaging (MRI) scanner, now used widely in hospitals, was developed at the medical school of the University of Aberdeen.

Use of the harbour and airport by the oil industry has given Aberdeen the title of 'oil capital of Europe'.

ABERDEEN, THE BEACH BALLROOM 1938 SA000012
(Courtesy of University of St Andrews Library)

More historical coin hoards have been found in Aberdeen than anywhere else. Hoards consist of large numbers of coins deliberately buried, perhaps at times of threat to the owners, and which for some reason were never recovered by the owners.

Aberdeen has won the Britain in Bloom competition more often than any other city.

ABERDEEN, THE BEACH AND THE BATHING STATION 1878 SA000026
(Courtesy of University of St Andrews Library)

ABERDEEN, SMOKING HADDIES 1902 SA000038

(Courtesy of University of St Andrews Library)

SEA-BEACH

ABERDEEN, CASTLE STREET 1878 SA000003

(Courtesy of University of St Andrews Library)

ABERDEEN 1892 A90302Z

ABERDEEN QUIZ QUESTIONS

1. Ptolemy, the 1st century cartographer, names a place on his map of the world which could be Aberdeen.
   What does he call it?

2. The Norse sagas mention the plundering of a town in the 11th century, which is almost certainly Aberdeen.
   What do they call this place?

3. St Machar, a 6th-century missionary, built his church where he found something for which he had been looking. Aberdeen's cathedral of St Machar stands on this site today. What was it he found?

4. A royal document of 1136 mentions which Aberdeen institution?

5. Aberdeen's oldest written charter was granted in 1179.
   Who granted it?

6. When Aberdeen's citizens gathered to attack an English garrison during the Wars of Independence, it is said that their password was 'bon accord'.
   What has become of this password?

7. The Great Charter of Robert the Bruce gave the burgh of Aberdeen something of great and lasting benefit.
   What was this?

8. The battle of Harlaw (1411) was remembered as an important event in Aberdeen's history.
   What was so important about it?

9. In 1495, Bishop Elphinstone, in consultation with the pope and King James IV, established an institution of immense importance to Aberdeen.
   What was it?

10. By 1528, Aberdeen had two examples of what were very unusual facilities in their day.
    What were they?

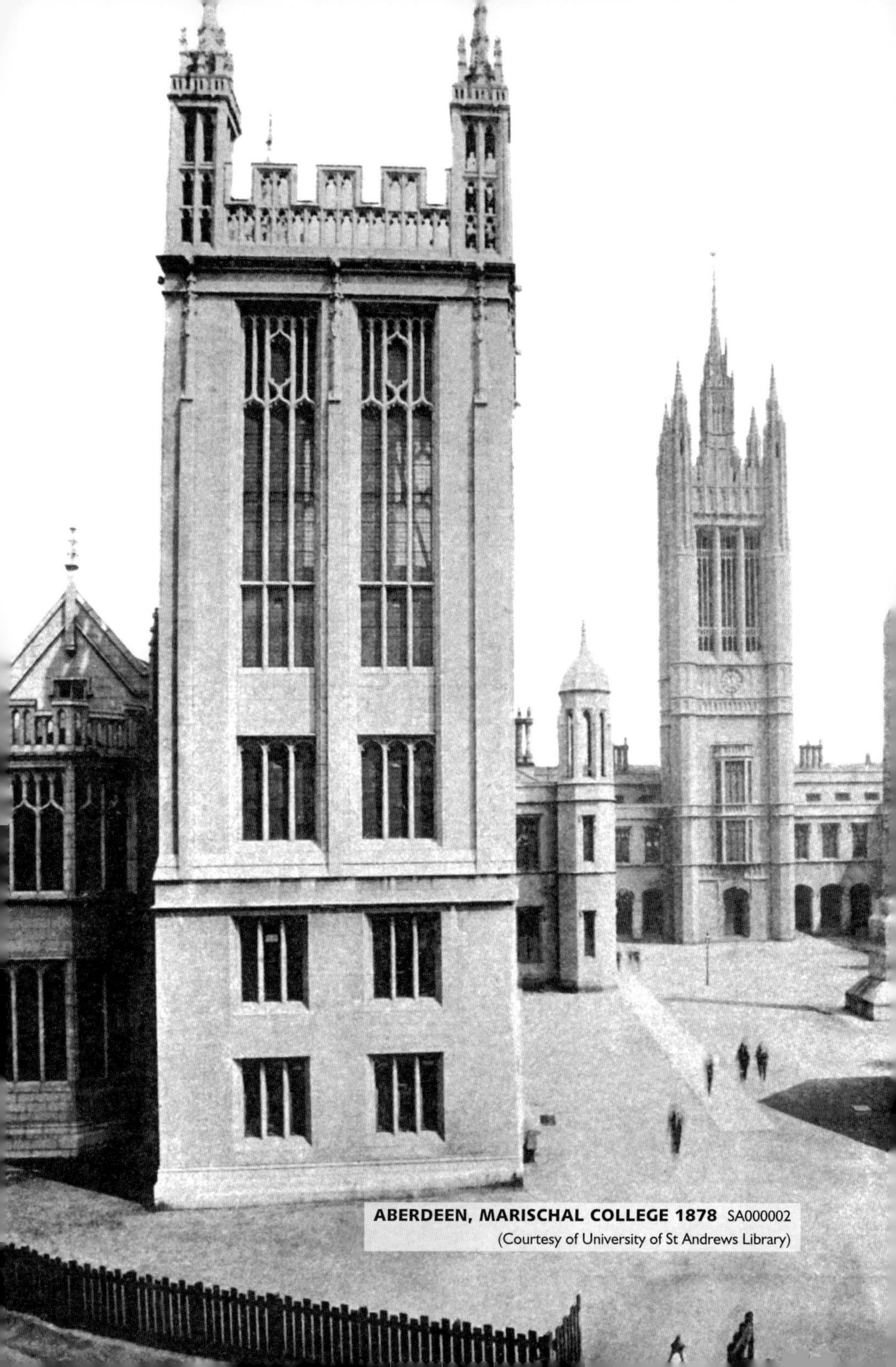

ABERDEEN, MARISCHAL COLLEGE 1878 SA000002
(Courtesy of University of St Andrews Library)

ABERDEEN, UNION BUILDINGS 1892 A90301v

11. By 1593, Aberdeen had two examples of something, at a time when the whole of England had only the same number. What were these?

12. Aberdonian George Jamesone was Scotland's earliest great painter.
What was he called by some of his admirers?

13. What was inflicted on Aberdeen in 1644 and is considered one of the greatest atrocities of the Civil War?

14. Between the 15th and 17th centuries, eleven provosts of Aberdeen were from the same family.
What was the family name?

15. An Aberdonian is usually reckoned to be one of Britain's greatest architects. (He designed St Martin-in-the-Fields in London).
What is his name?

ABERDEEN, FROM ABOVE THE SUSPENSION BRIDGE c1885 A90303

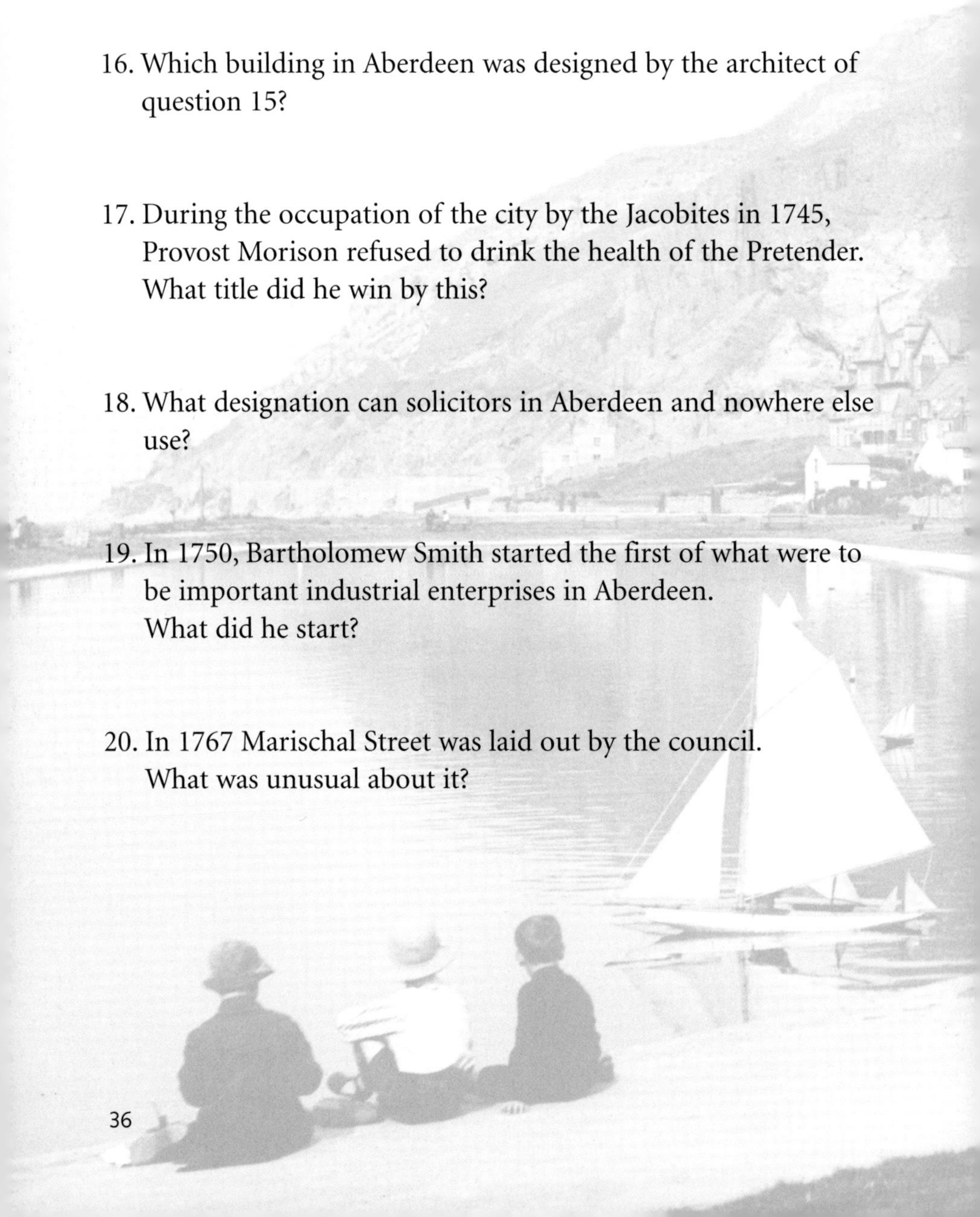

16. Which building in Aberdeen was designed by the architect of question 15?

17. During the occupation of the city by the Jacobites in 1745, Provost Morison refused to drink the health of the Pretender. What title did he win by this?

18. What designation can solicitors in Aberdeen and nowhere else use?

19. In 1750, Bartholomew Smith started the first of what were to be important industrial enterprises in Aberdeen.
What did he start?

20. In 1767 Marischal Street was laid out by the council.
What was unusual about it?

ABERDEEN, THE SOUTH KIRK AND THE MITHER KIRK c1900 SA000006
(Courtesy of University of St Andrews Library)

ABERDEEN, THE QUEEN'S MONUMENT PRE 1873 SA000008
(Courtesy of University of St Andrews Library)

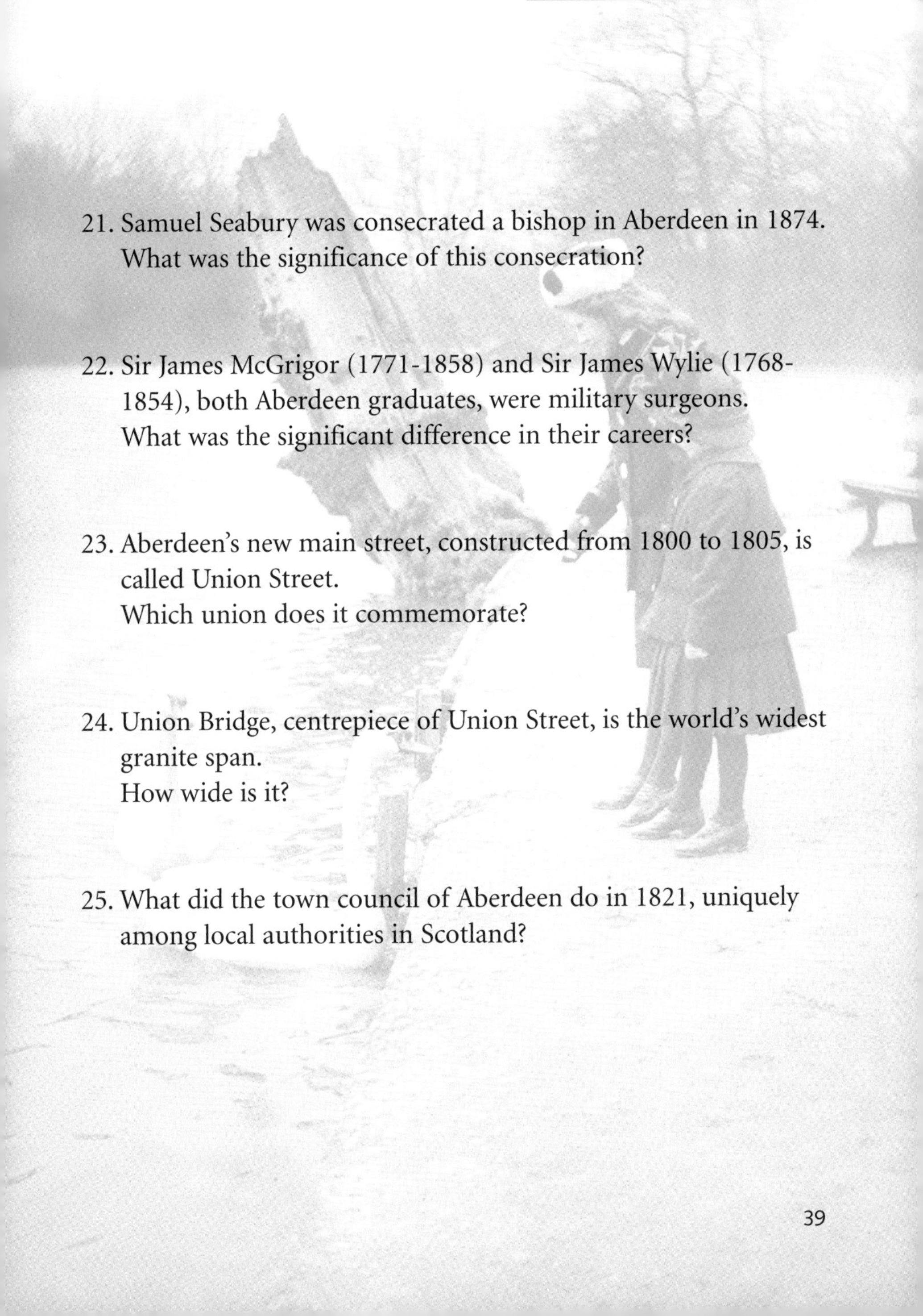

21. Samuel Seabury was consecrated a bishop in Aberdeen in 1874. What was the significance of this consecration?

22. Sir James McGrigor (1771-1858) and Sir James Wylie (1768-1854), both Aberdeen graduates, were military surgeons. What was the significant difference in their careers?

23. Aberdeen's new main street, constructed from 1800 to 1805, is called Union Street. Which union does it commemorate?

24. Union Bridge, centrepiece of Union Street, is the world's widest granite span. How wide is it?

25. What did the town council of Aberdeen do in 1821, uniquely among local authorities in Scotland?

26. After experiments with models in a tank of water, the Aberdeen company Alexander Hall and Co built the first of the Scottish clipper ships. What was she called?

27. In 1859, Walter Hood and Co built the fastest of all clipper ships. What was she called?

ABERDEEN, BRIG O' BALGOWNIE c**1890** A90304

ABERDEEN, UNION STREET c1885 A90305

28. A man educated in Old Aberdeen arranged for Alexander Hall and Co to build what were to become the first ships in the Japanese navy. Who was he?

29. The railway reached Aberdeen from the south in 1850. From which place are the mile-posts numbered?

30. Aberdeen's own railway company was called the Great North of Scotland Railway.
What was remarkable about this name?

31. Aberdonian artist William Dyce died before completing a major commission.
What was he painting?

ABERDEEN, ST NICHOLAS STREET AND QUEEN'S CORNER c1899 A90307

ABERDEEN, WALLACE STATUE 1935 SA000017
(Courtesy of University of St Andrews Library)

32. The pioneer photographer George Washington Wilson of Aberdeen took the first photograph of something which has been photographed millions of times since.
What did he photograph?

33. Aberdeen Town Council established works twenty miles west of the city at Invercannie in 1866.
What was supplied?

34. Aberdeen's first public park was established next to the railway line. What was its popular name?

35. 'Toiler' came to Aberdeen in 1882.
Why was this important?

36. Aberdeen exported thousands of tons of granite every year to cities all over Britain, plus several cites in Europe.
In what form was this granite exported?

37. A tunnel under the streets of Aberdeen is the longest such structure in the world.
What does it contain?

38. Apart from Queen Victoria, Aberdeen has only two female statues. Both are Greek.
Who are they?

39. Three important public buildings stand alone on a prominent site in the centre of Aberdeen.
As what are they popularly known?

40. The first example of an important medical machine in Britain was built in Aberdeen's City Hospital in 1933. Some of these machines were to be in use for fifty years.
What was it?

41. A Luftwaffe aeroplane was escorted into Dyce Airport in Aberdeen in 1943.
Why?

ABERDEEN, GUILD STREET 1880 SA000027
(Courtesy of University of St Andrews Library)

ABERDEEN, UNION TERRACE AND GARDENS c**1915** A90308

42. An Aberdonian woman retired to her native city after a spectacular career as an opera singer and impresario, mainly in the USA.
Who was she?

43. A scientist whose reputation was made at the Rowett Research Institute at Aberdeen was appointed in 1945 to head the UN Food and Agriculture Organisation. He won the Nobel Peace Prize in 1949.
Who was he?

44. What ended in Aberdeen in 1958 after eighty-four years of service?

45. A new medical machine was developed by the medical school in Aberdeen to replace and improve on X-rays. What was it?

ABERDEEN, THE BRIDGE OF DEE c1900 A90310

46. Aberdeen has a popular name derived from its most visible characteristic. What is it?

ABERDEEN, MARKET CROSS 1892 A90302

ABERDEEN, ST MARY'S ROMAN CATHOLIC CATHEDRAL 1889 SA000032

(Courtesy of University of St Andrews Library)

47. The city established another name for itself to promote the holiday trade.
What was it?

48. Recent industrial developments have added yet another name for Aberdeen since the 1970s.
What is this?

ABERDEEN, REGENT'S QUAY 1878 SA000001
(Courtesy of University of St Andrews Library)

49. What title has Aberdeen won more often than any other city - so often that at one time it was banned from the competition to give others a chance?

50. What are found more frequently in Aberdeen than in any other city during archaeological digs?

ABERDEEN, THE SOUTH BREAKWATER 1935 SA000011
(Courtesy of University of St Andrews Library)

ABERDEEN, THE BRIDGE OF DON 1938 SA000010
(Courtesy of University of St Andrews Library)

ABERDEEN QUIZ ANSWERS

1. Devana.

2. Apardion.

3. A river bending in the shape of a shepherd's crook.

4. Aberdeen Harbour Board.

5. King William the Lion.

6. It is now the city's motto.

7. The Freedom Lands, over which the council are superiors.

8. Provost Sir Robert Davidson died leading the citizens into the battle.

9. King's College, Aberdeen's first university.

10. Bridges over major rivers.

11. Universities.

12. The Scottish van Dyck.

13. A massacre of civilians by Cromwell's New Model Army.

14. Menzies.

15. James Gibbs.

16. The West Kirk of St Nicholas.

17. Provost Positive.

18. Advocate in Aberdeen.

19.The paper mill at Peterculter, now within the city boundary.

20. Its whole length was on a viaduct.

21. He was the first overseas bishop of the Anglican communion.

22. Sir James McGrigor served in the British Army: Sir James Wylie served in the Russian Army.

23. The Union of the Parliaments of Great Britain and Ireland.

24. 130 feet.

25. The city declared itself bankrupt.

26. 'Scottish Maid'.

27. 'Thermopylae'.

ABERDEEN QUIZ ANSWERS

28. Thomas Blake Glover.

29. Carlisle.

30. It was the smallest of the Scottish railway companies and the smallest railway company to have 'Great' in its name.

31. Murals in the Robing Room at the Palace of Westminster.

32. The Moon.

33. Clean water.

34. The Trainy Park.

35. She was the first trawler to work from the port and so the initiator of the city's status as the greatest fishing port.

36. Causeway setts for paving streets.

37. Mains electricity cables.

38. Demeter and Hygeia. Demeter is on the bank building known as The Hinge of the City, (now a pub), and Hygeia is on the obelisk commemorating Sir James Macgrigor now in Duthie Park.

39. The buildings are: the central library (education), the South Free Kirk (salvation) and the theatre (damnation).

40. An iron lung.

41. The pilot was defecting with the secret 'Liechtenstein' equipment aboard.

42. Mary Garden.

43. Dr - later Lord - John Boyd Orr.

44. The trams.

45. The magnetic resonance imaging scanner (MRI scanner).

46. The Granite City.

47. The silver city with the golden sands.

48. The oil capital of Europe.

49. Winner of Britain in Bloom.

50. Coin hoards.

GOUDHURST, MEASURING THE HOPS 1904 52571

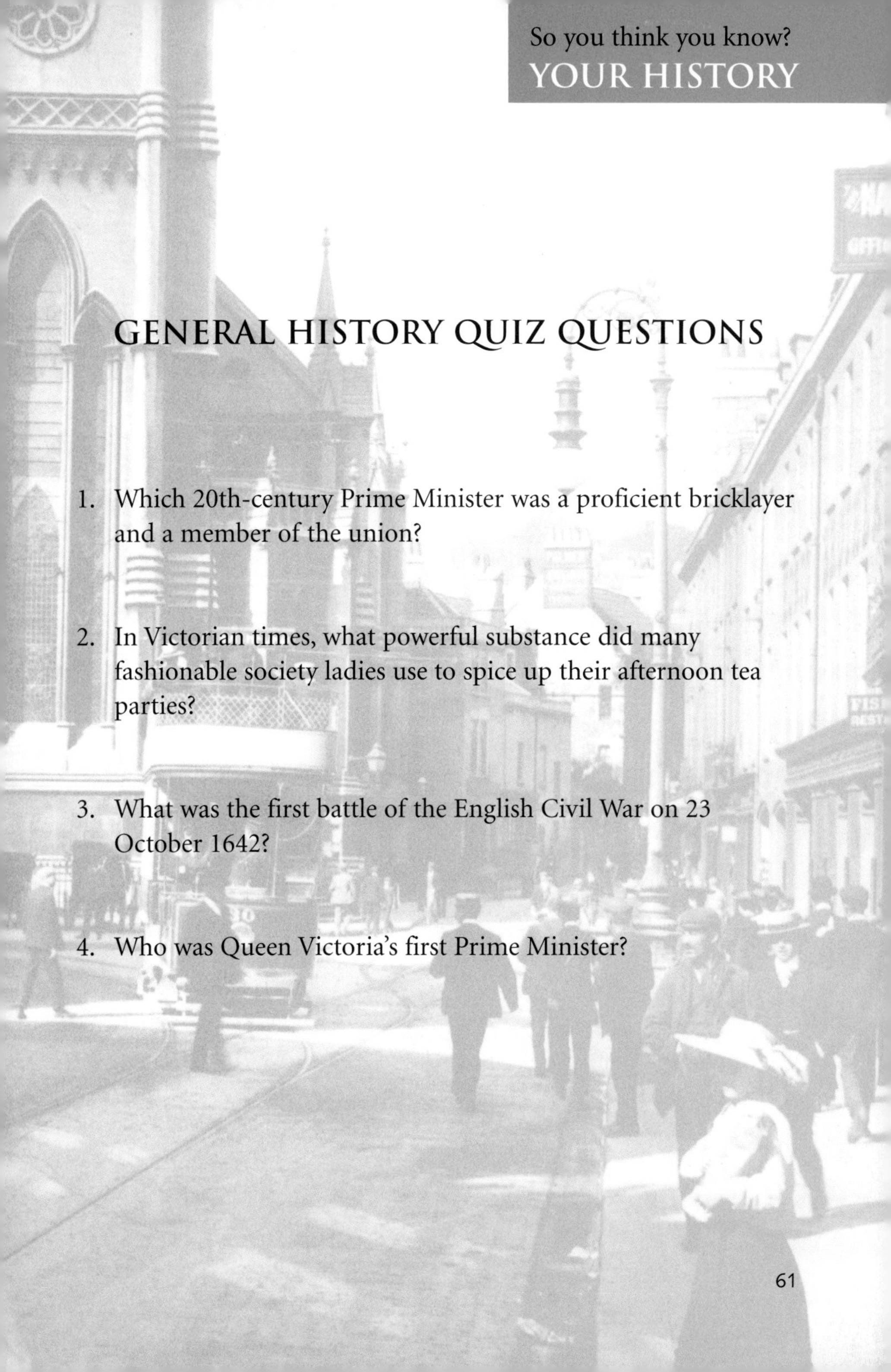

GENERAL HISTORY QUIZ QUESTIONS

1. Which 20th-century Prime Minister was a proficient bricklayer and a member of the union?

2. In Victorian times, what powerful substance did many fashionable society ladies use to spice up their afternoon tea parties?

3. What was the first battle of the English Civil War on 23 October 1642?

4. Who was Queen Victoria's first Prime Minister?

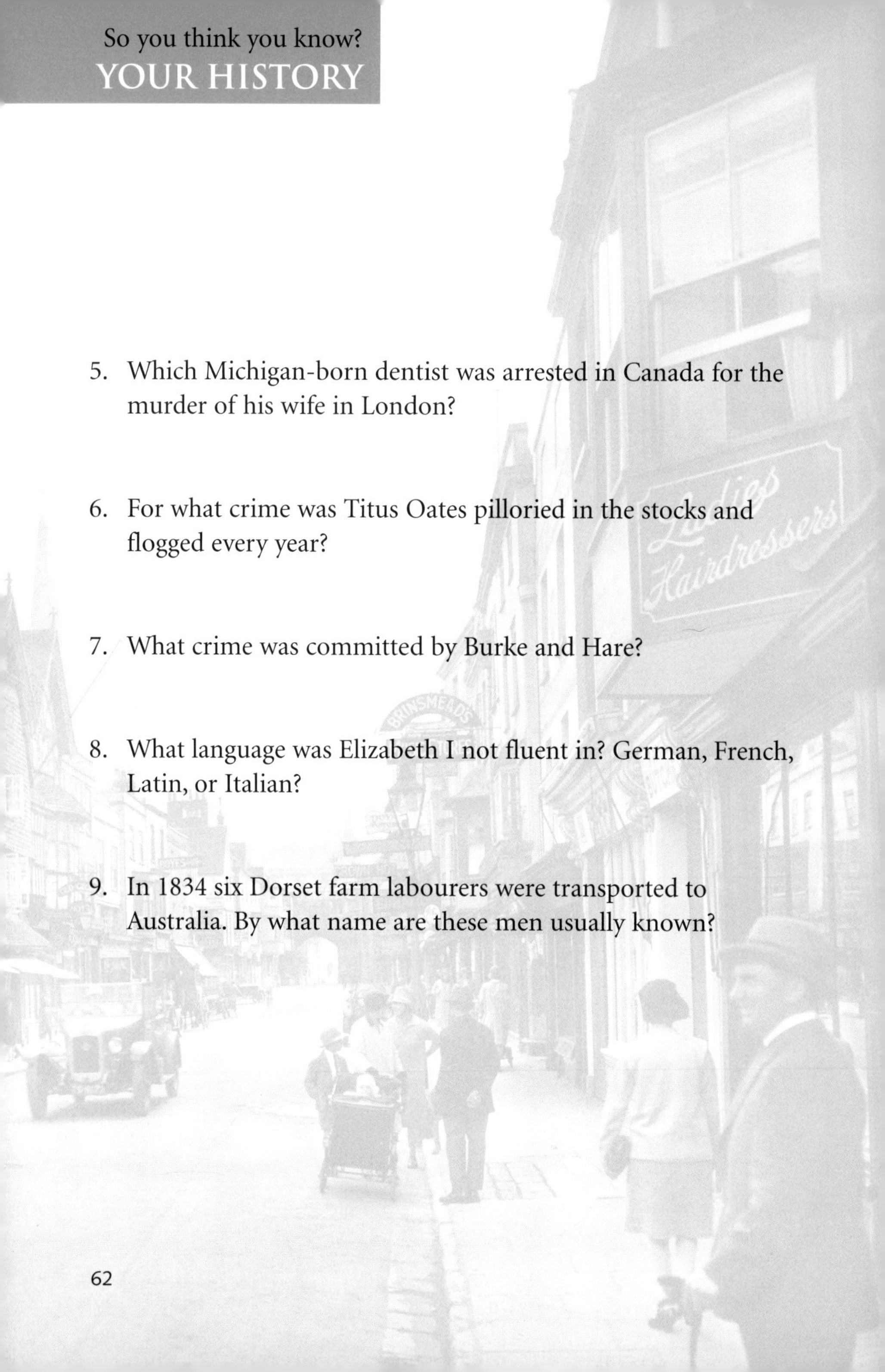

5. Which Michigan-born dentist was arrested in Canada for the murder of his wife in London?

6. For what crime was Titus Oates pilloried in the stocks and flogged every year?

7. What crime was committed by Burke and Hare?

8. What language was Elizabeth I not fluent in? German, French, Latin, or Italian?

9. In 1834 six Dorset farm labourers were transported to Australia. By what name are these men usually known?

HORNING, ON THE BROADS 1902 48108

MARKET DRAYTON, MARKET DAY 1911 63338

10. At which battle was Richard III slain?

11. Who was the first Prime Minister to live at Chequers?

12. Who was the leader of the Women's Social and Political Union?

13. What year were women granted the vote on the Isle of Man?
1881, 1902, 1912, or 1946?

RHYL, DONKEYS ON THE SANDS 1891 29151

14. Which king signed the Magna Carta in 1215 at Runnymede?

15. In which city was the infamous Peterloo Massacre on 16 August 1819?

16. Who were the mother and father of Elizabeth I?

17. Before the French Revolution in 1789, who is reported to have said 'Let them eat cake'?

18. Who wore two shirts in which to be executed, and why?

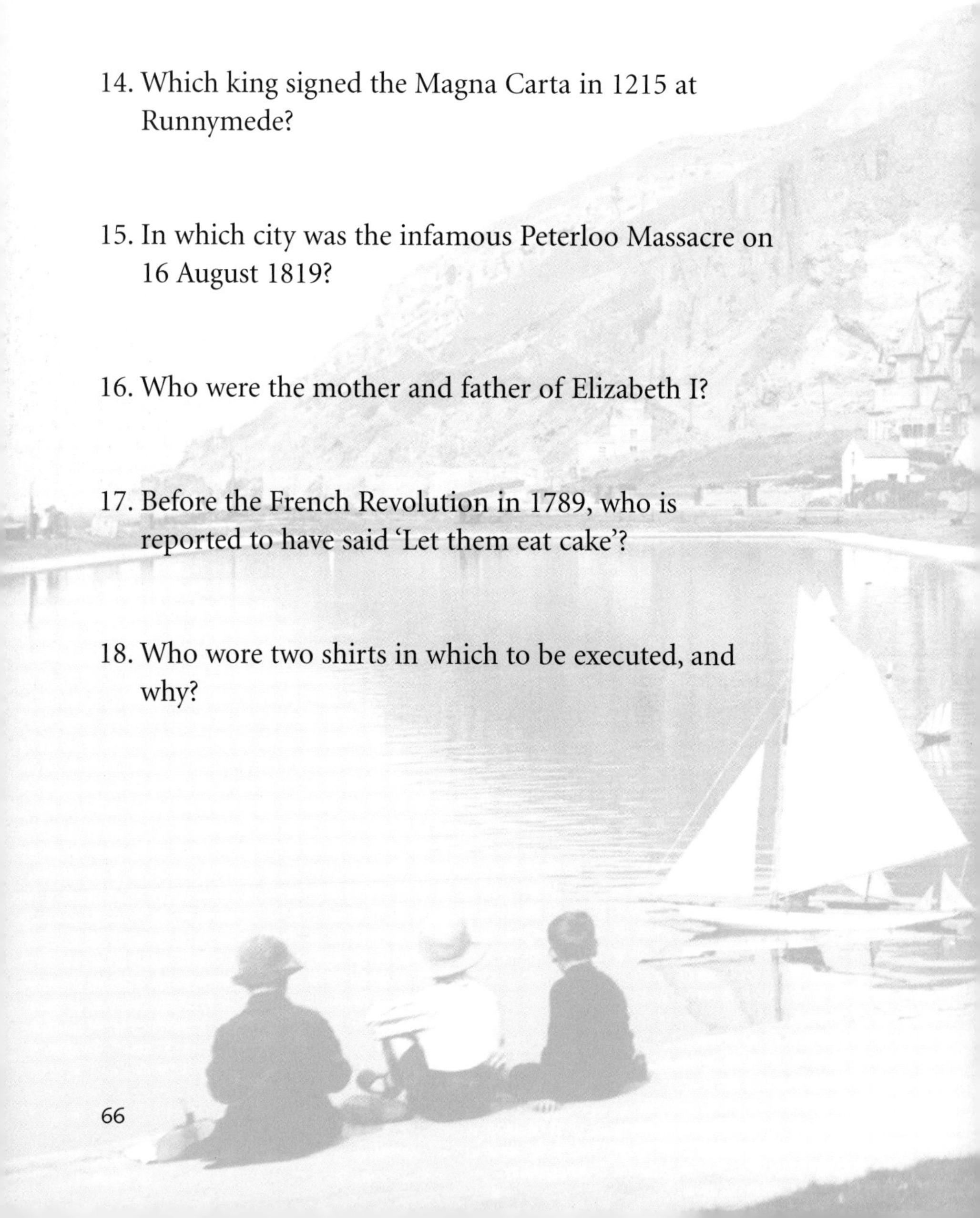

SHANKLIN, THE STAGECOACHES 1913 66211A

NEWQUAY, THE HARBOUR 1894 33522

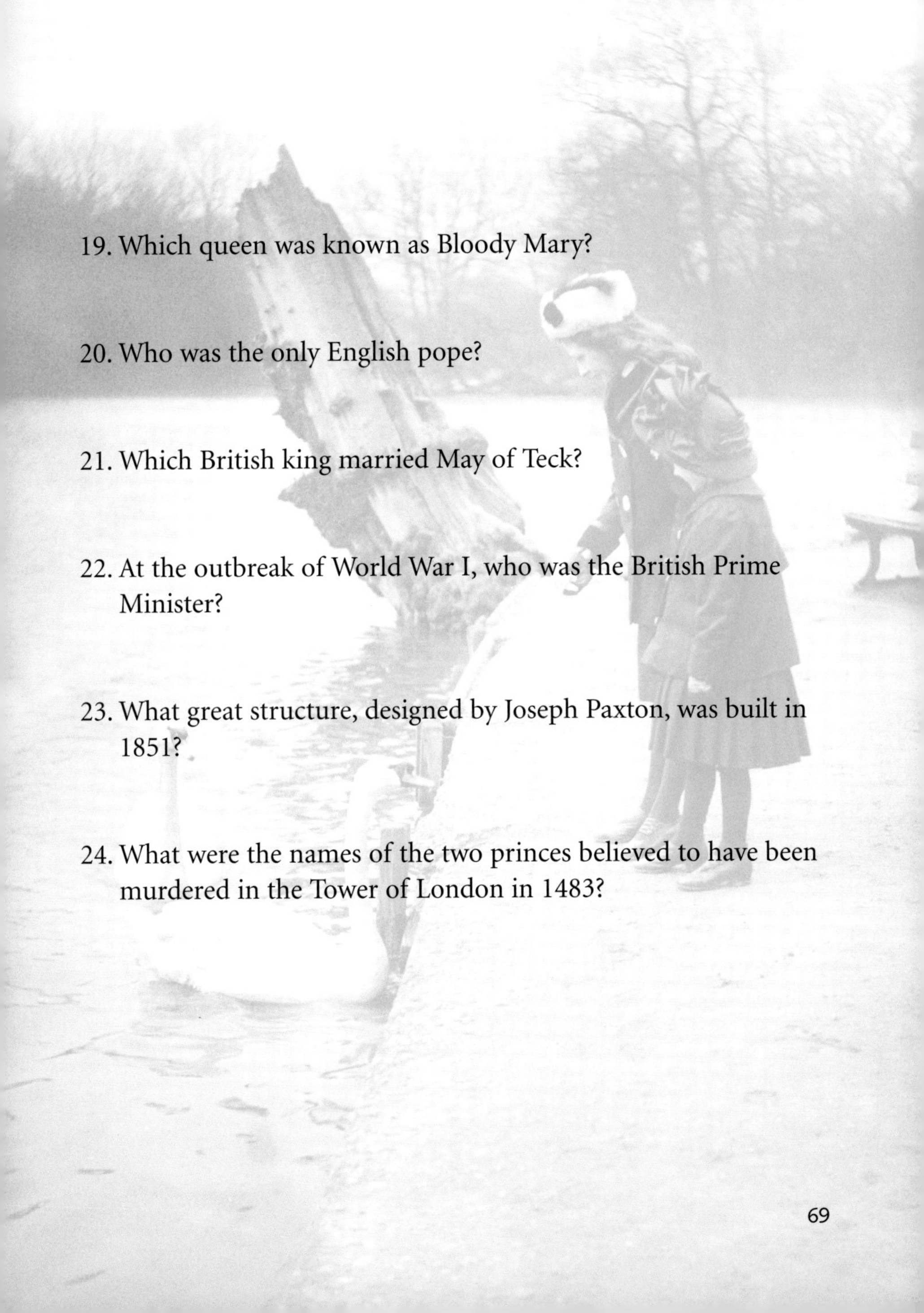

19. Which queen was known as Bloody Mary?

20. Who was the only English pope?

21. Which British king married May of Teck?

22. At the outbreak of World War I, who was the British Prime Minister?

23. What great structure, designed by Joseph Paxton, was built in 1851?

24. What were the names of the two princes believed to have been murdered in the Tower of London in 1483?

25. What unusual accident eventually caused the death of the Prince of Wales, eldest son of George II?

26. Which of Dickens's novels depicts the struggles and strife of factory workers in Victorian England?

EVERSLEY, THE WHITE HART 1906 57011

CASTLETON, SPEEDWELL CAVERN 1909 61785

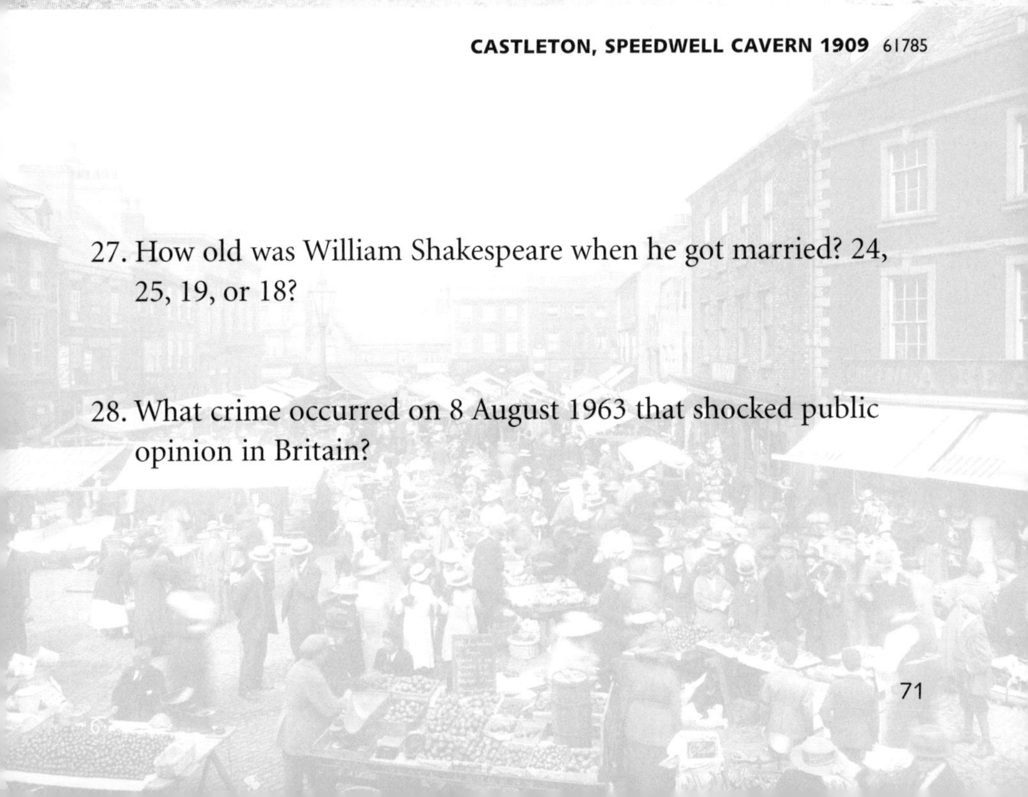

27. How old was William Shakespeare when he got married? 24, 25, 19, or 18?

28. What crime occurred on 8 August 1963 that shocked public opinion in Britain?

29. Who had to hide in an oak tree to save his life after a military defeat?

30. After Henry VIII's Dissolution of the Monasteries, what are some of the new owners of the monastery buildings rumoured to have done with some of the illuminated manuscripts they found?

KING'S LYNN, HIGH STREET 1908 60023

BOURNEMOUTH, INVALID'S WALK 1900 45226

31. In July 1888, 1,500 female employees went on strike at a factory at Bow in East London. What did they manufacture?

32. Who was the Irish saint who legend says saw the Loch Ness Monster in Scotland?
St Columba, St Patrick, St Andrew, or St Aidan?

33. Which English woman made this prophecy:
'Carriages without horses shall go, And accidents fill the world with woe. Around the world thoughts shall fly, In the twinkling of an eye.'?

34. Which tax was levied between 1696 and 1851?

35. How long did the Hundred Years' War last? 116 years, 94 years, 100 years, or 108 years?

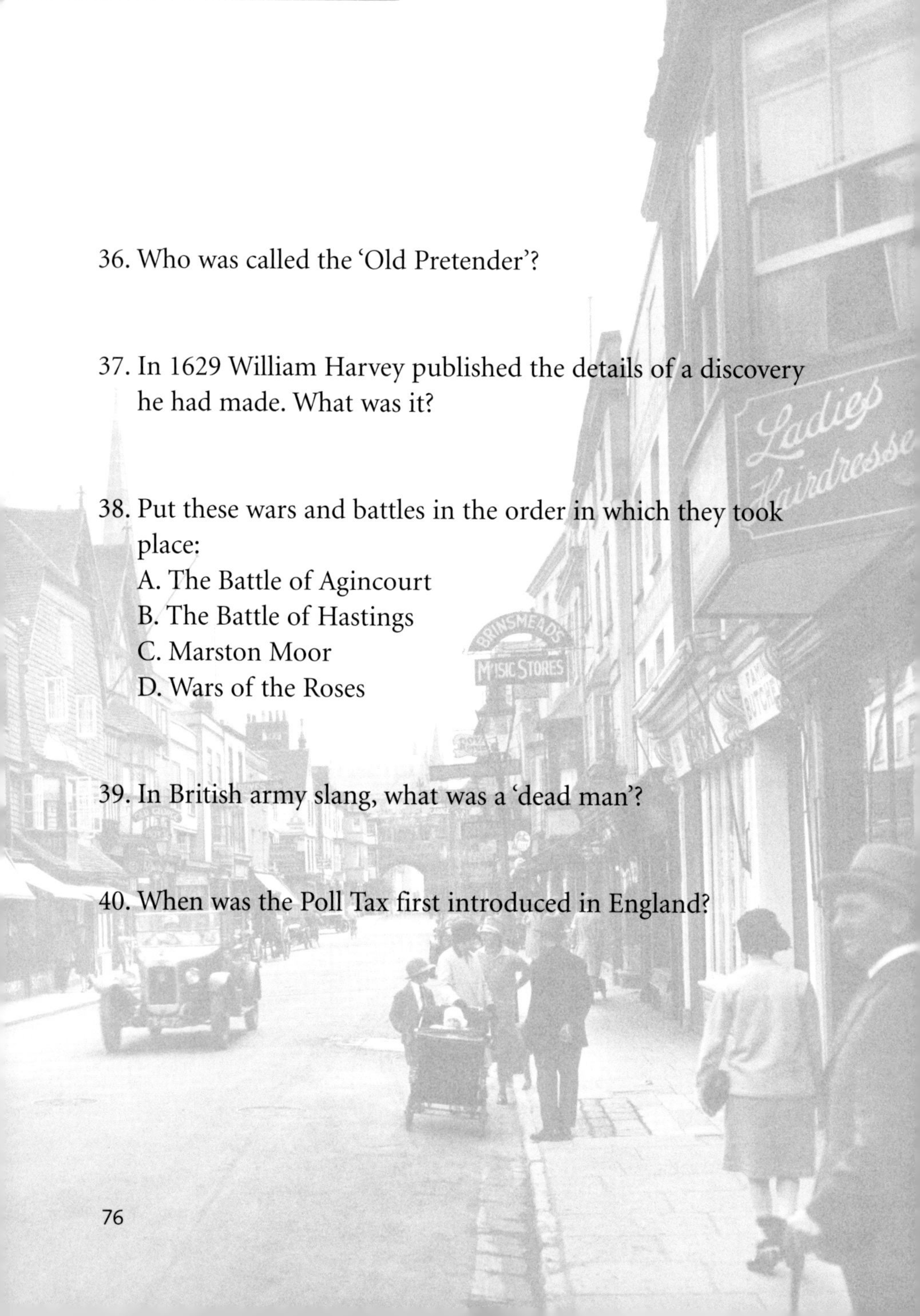

36. Who was called the ‘Old Pretender’?

37. In 1629 William Harvey published the details of a discovery he had made. What was it?

38. Put these wars and battles in the order in which they took place:
A. The Battle of Agincourt
B. The Battle of Hastings
C. Marston Moor
D. Wars of the Roses

39. In British army slang, what was a ‘dead man’?

40. When was the Poll Tax first introduced in England?

SAFFRON WALDEN, FRY'S GARDEN 1907 58821

CLOVELLY, POST OFFICE, TRANSFER OF MAIL 1936 87551

41. Who was the first Prime Minister of Britain?

42. What is pannage?

43. What were the Welshmen of the Rebecca Riots, who dressed up as women, protesting against?

44. How many people did the 1715 Riot Act have to be read to, in order for them to be guilty of a felony, and liable to the punishment of death? 6, 12, 27, or 250?

CHALFORD, THE VILLAGE 1910 62713

45. What was the joint stock company, the South Sea Company, set up in 1711 to trade in?

46. In the Middle Ages, a split stick was used by royal officials to record sums of money paid. Notches were cut on it representing payments. What was it called?

EASTBOURNE, THE PIER 1925 77946

WEYMOUTH, THE SANDS 1909 61597

47. When did the Union Jack achieve its present pattern?

48. In 1752, September 2 was followed by September 14. What was the name of the new calendar system that involved this adjustment?

NEWBY BRIDGE, THE SWAN HOTEL 1914 67414

49. Coffee houses were patronised by literary giants such as Dryden, Johnson, and Pope. How many coffee houses were there in London in the 18th century?
10, 50, 250, or 1800?

50. Who was the first British Prime Minister to live at 10 Downing Street?

TENBY 1890 28091

GENERAL HISTORY QUIZ ANSWERS

1. Winston Churchill.
2. Opium.
3. Edgehill.
4. Lord Melbourne.
5. Dr Crippen. He buried her body in the basement of his London house.
6. For giving false evidence against Catholics.
7. They murdered people and sold their corpses to unscrupulous surgeons for dissection.
8. German.
9. The Tolpuddle Martyrs.
10. The Battle of Bosworth Field.
11. Lloyd George.
12. Emmeline Pankhurst.
13. 1881.

14. King John.

15. Manchester.

16. Henry VIII and Anne Boleyn.

17. Marie Antoinette.

18. Charles I. The weather was cold and he did not want to be seen shivering.

19. Mary I, the daughter of Henry VIII and Catherine of Aragon. She married Philip II of Spain, and was a devout Catholic. She earned her nickname from her persecution of Protestants.

20. Adrian IV, born Nicholas Brakespeare in 1100.

21. George V (she was known in this country as Mary).

22. Herbert Asquith.

23. The Crystal Palace.

24. Edward V and his brother Richard Duke of York, the sons of Edward IV.

25. He was hit on the head by a cricket ball.

GENERAL HISTORY QUIZ ANSWERS

26. 'Hard Times', published in 1854.

27. 18.

28. The Great Train Robbery.

29. Charles II.

30. They used them as lavatory paper.

31. Matches. They worked at the Bryant and May factory.

32. St Columba, born cAD521.

33. Mother Shipton, born in Norfolk in 1485.

34. Window Tax, which was payable on a house with more than six windows.

35. 116 years, between 1337 and 1453.

36. James III (the son of James II). In 1715 he gathered together a force of 10,000 men and invaded England. The Jacobites fought their way as far as Preston, where they were dispersed.

37. The circulation of the blood. He was physician extraordinary to James I.

38. B (1066) A (1415) D (1455-85) C (1644).

39. An empty bottle.

40. In 1222, on every person over the age of 14.

41. Robert Walpole. As first Lord of the Treasury between 1721 and 1742 he presided over the cabinet.

42. The right of tenants to graze their swine in the woods of a manor.

43. They destroyed turnpike houses, being unhappy about the levels of tolls.

44. 12.

45. Slaves in Latin America.

46. A tally.

47. In 1801, when the cross of St Patrick was added to the crosses of St George and St Andrew.

48. The Gregorian Calendar.

49. 1800.

50. Sir Robert Walpole (1676-1745).

Ottakar's Bookshops

Ottakar's bookshops, the first of which opened in Brighton in 1988, can now be found in over 130 towns and cities across the United Kingdom. Expansion was gradual throughout the 1990s, but the chain has expanded rapidly in recent years, with many new shop openings and the acquisition of shops from James Thin and Hammicks.

Ottakar's has always known that a shop's local profile is as important, if not more important, than the chain's national profile, and has encouraged its staff to make their shops a part of the local community, tailoring stock to suit the area and forging links with local schools and businesses.

Local history has always been a strong area for Ottakar's, and the company has published its own award winning local history titles, based on text written by its customers, in recent years.

With a reputation for friendly, intelligent and enthusiastic booksellers, warm, inviting shops with an excellent range of books and related products, Ottakar's is now one of the UK's most popular booksellers. In 2003 and then again in 2004 it won the prestigious Best Bookselling Company of the Year Award at the British Book Awards.

Ottakar's has commissioned The Francis Frith Collection to create a series of town history books similar to this volume, as well as a range of stylish gift products, all illustrated with historical photographs.

Participating Ottakar's bookshops can be found in the following towns and cities:

Aberdeen
Abergavenny
Aberystwyth
Andover
Ashford
Ayr
Banbury
Barnstaple
Basildon
Berkhamsted
Bishop's Stortford
Boston
Brentwood
Bromley
Bury St Edmunds
Camberley
Canterbury
Carmarthen
Chatham
Chelmsford
Cheltenham
Cirencester
Coventry
Crawley
Darlington
Dorchester
Douglas, Isle of Man
Dumfries
Dundee
East Grinstead
Eastbourne
Elgin
Enfield
Epsom
Falkirk
Fareham
Farnham
Folkestone
Glasgow
Gloucester
Greenwich
Grimsby
Guildford
Harrogate
Hastings
Haywards Heath
Hemel Hempstead
High Wycombe
Horsham
Huddersfield
Inverness
Isle of Wight
Kendal
King's Lynn
Kirkcaldy
Lancaster
Lincoln
Llandudno
Loughborough
Lowestoft
Luton
Lymington
Maidenhead
Maidstone
Market Harborough
Milton Keynes
Newport
Newton Abbot
Norwich
Oban
Ormskirk
Petersfield
Portsmouth
Poole
Redhill
St Albans
St Andrews
St Neots
St Helier
Salisbury
Sheffield
Stafford
Staines
Stevenage
Sutton Coldfield
Teddington
Tenterden
Tiverton
Torquay
Trowbridge
Truro
Tunbridge Wells
Twickenham
Walsall
Wilmslow and
Alderley Edge
Wells
Weston-super-Mare
Windsor
Witney
Woking
Worcester
Yeovil

Francis Frith

Pioneer Victorian Photographer

Francis Frith, founder of the world-famous photographic archive, was a complex and multi-talented man. A devout Quaker and a highly successful Victorian businessman, he was philosophical by nature and pioneering in outlook. By 1855 he had already established a wholesale grocery business in Liverpool, and sold it for the astonishing sum of £200,000, which is the equivalent today of over £15,000,000. Now in his thirties, and captivated by the new science of photography, Frith set out on a series of pioneering journeys up the Nile and to the Near East.

INTRIGUE AND EXPLORATION

He was the first photographer to venture beyond the sixth cataract of the Nile. Africa was still the mysterious 'Dark Continent', and Stanley and Livingstone's historic meeting was a decade into the future. The conditions for picture taking confound belief. He laboured for hours in his wicker dark-room in the sweltering heat of the desert, while the volatile chemicals fizzed dangerously in their trays. Back in London he exhibited his photographs and was 'rapturously cheered' by members of the Royal Society. His reputation as a photographer was made overnight.

VENTURE OF A LIFE-TIME

By the 1870s the railways had threaded their way across the country, and Bank Holidays and half-day Saturdays had been made obligatory by Act of Parliament. All of a sudden the working man and his family were able to enjoy days out, take holidays, and see a little more of the world.

With typical business acumen, Francis Frith foresaw that these new tourists would enjoy having souvenirs to commemorate their days out. For the next thirty years he travelled the country by train and by pony and trap, producing fine photographs of seaside resorts and beauty spots that were keenly bought by millions of Victorians. These prints were painstakingly pasted into family albums and pored over during the dark nights of winter, rekindling precious memories of summer excursions. Frith's studio was soon supplying retail shops all over the country, and by 1890 F Frith & Co had become the greatest specialist photographic publishing company in the world, with over 2,000 sales outlets, and pioneered the picture postcard.

FRANCIS FRITH'S LEGACY

Francis Frith had died in 1898 at his villa in Cannes, his great project still growing. By 1970 the archive he created contained over a third of a million pictures showing 7,000 British towns and villages.

Frith's legacy to us today is of immense significance and value, for the magnificent archive of evocative photographs he created provides a unique record of change in the cities, towns and villages throughout Britain over a century and more. Frith and his fellow studio photographers revisited locations many times down the years to update their views, compiling for us an enthralling and colourful pageant of British life and character.

We are fortunate that Frith was dedicated to recording the minutiae of everyday life. For it is this sheer wealth of visual data, the painstaking chronicle of changes in dress, transport, street layouts, buildings, housing and landscape that captivates us so much today, offering us a powerful link with the past and with the lives of our ancestors.

Computers have now made it possible for Frith's many thousands of images to be accessed almost instantly. The archive offers every one of us an opportunity to examine the places where we and our families have lived and worked down the years. Its images, depicting our shared past, are now bringing pleasure and enlightenment to millions around the world a century and more after his death.

For further information visit: www.francisfrith.co.uk